CHALK AROUND THE BLOCK

by Sharon McKay and David

Illustrations by Marilyn M

Somerville House Publishing

Toronto

Text and Illustration Copyright © 1993 by Somerville House Books Limited

Canadian Cataloguing in Publication Data

McKay, Sharon.
      Chalk around the block

ISBN 0-921051-81-6.

1. Games. I. Macleod, David, 1953-
II. Mets, Marilyn. III. Title.

GV1203.M3 1993   j796.2   C92-095530-4

Printed in China

Package Design by M & Y, Inc.
Book Design by Marilyn Mets.

Published simultaneously in the United States by Andrews and McMeel.

Published in Canada by: Somerville House Publishing,
                            a division of Somerville House Books Limited,
                            3080 Yonge Street, Suite 5000,
                            Toronto, Ontario.
                            M4N 3N1

Dedication:
To Sam, Joe and Nichole.

CONTENTS

WHAT IS CHALK?

Today we call it chalk. The ancient Romans called it "creta." There was a time in the early history of life on the earth that so much creta, or chalk, was formed that we now call that time the Cretaceous period — the time of chalk.

The Cretaceous period began about 135 million years ago and lasted almost 60 million years — the time of dinosaurs.

Chalk is made up of the remains of tiny sea creatures that lived during the Cretaceous period. They were so small that you would have needed a microscope to see them. Over millions of years their shells formed into thick layers on the sea bottom. If you think of each tiny shell as a snowflake, and the Cretaceous period as one long snowstorm, you can imagine how thick layers of chalk formed. However, the

shells were much smaller than snowflakes and they didn't melt. That is why chalk is still with us today.

Over the years chalk has had many uses. It has long been used as an ingredient in cosmetics. Renaissance artists used natural red and black chalk in their drawings. It has been used in toothpaste and in making cement and for fertilizer. But chalk's best known use is as a writing tool.

So strap on your chalk and get set to take a CHALK AROUND THE BLOCK.

BEFORE WE START

CHALK SAFETY TIP

If you play on the driveway, draw two lines at the base of it. The first line is the line **WARNING** your friends and little brothers and sisters.

Explain to them that they are not to cross this line. The second line, closer to the road, is the **EMERGENCY STOP** line that must never be crossed when playing.

The games in this book are played on large, medium, and small hard surfaces.

Examples are:
large — a paved schoolyard or vacant parking lot.

medium — a paved or cement driveway.
small — a cement garage floor, basement floor, or driveway.

Cement garage and basement floors are excellent hard-tops on hot days. The roof gives shelter from a blazing sun and the natural dampness keeps everyone cool.

CONVERSION TABLES

Here are some common measurements used in this book. Most measurements for the games don't have to be exact. Close is good enough.

Imperial/US	Metric	Approximate Other
1 inch =	2.5 centimeters (cm) =	distance from knuckle to fingernail on your index finger.
6 inches =	15 cm =	length of your shoe.
1 foot =	30 cm =	length of two shoes heel-to-toe.
3 feet (1 yard) =	1 meter =	1 big stretching step.
15 feet =	5 meters =	5 big stretching steps.

SIDEWALK ART

Try the chalk that came with this book on this page to get used to using it. Try blending two colors to create a third. If there is a sidewalk in front of your home, and with your parent's or caregiver's permission, you can draw great pictures in chalk. Go outside and draw a picture of your home. Or draw a long chalk dragon down the sidewalk. Name it, if you wish.

THE LITTLE BALL

Age: Toddlers

Players: 1 or more and parent or caregiver

Materials: Chalk and ball, bean bag, or pebble

• Draw a circle 2 feet (2/3 meter) across on a small surface.

• Everyone should take a turn rolling the ball into the circle. When the ball stops in the circle, sing (to the tune of "London Bridge"):

"The ball has rolled into the ring,
Let us clap and let us sing.
Let us clap and let us sing
The ball has rolled into the ring."

• If the ball keeps rolling out of the circle, use a small pebble or bean bag instead.

DID YOU KNOW that this game is very popular in Mexico?

MARBLE SHOOT

Age: 5 and up
Players: 2 or more
Materials: Chalk and marbles

• Draw a start line on a small surface.

• Player 1 shoots a marble from behind the start line.

• Player 2 shoots a marble and attempts to hit player 1's marble. If she hits it, she keeps it. If she misses it, it's player 3's turn. (If there are only two players, then it's player 1's turn again.)

• This player may shoot at either marble. If he hits either one, he keeps it and shoots again. He keeps shooting until he misses or has won all the marbles. If no marbles are left on the ground the next player shoots one out and the game continues.

• The game is over when one player has captured all the other players' marbles or when the players decide to end the game. Whoever has the most marbles at the end of the game wins.

SHOOT OUT

Age: 5 and up
Players: 2 or more
Materials: Chalk and marbles

• On a small surface, draw a circle about 3 feet (1 meter) across. In the center of the circle, draw one 6 inches (15 cm) across.

• Each player places the same number of marbles inside the small circle keeping one marble as a "shooter."

• Each player tries to knock one or more of the marbles in the small circle outside of the large circle.

• Player 1 shoots from outside the big circle. If player 1 succeeds, she shoots again from where her shooter landed. She continues to shoot until she fails to knock a marble outside of the large circle. When this happens (even if the shooter has gone outside the large circle), it's the next player's turn.

• Each player captures the marbles that she has knocked outside the large circle.

• The game is over when all of the marbles have been knocked out.

• The player with the most captured marbles wins.

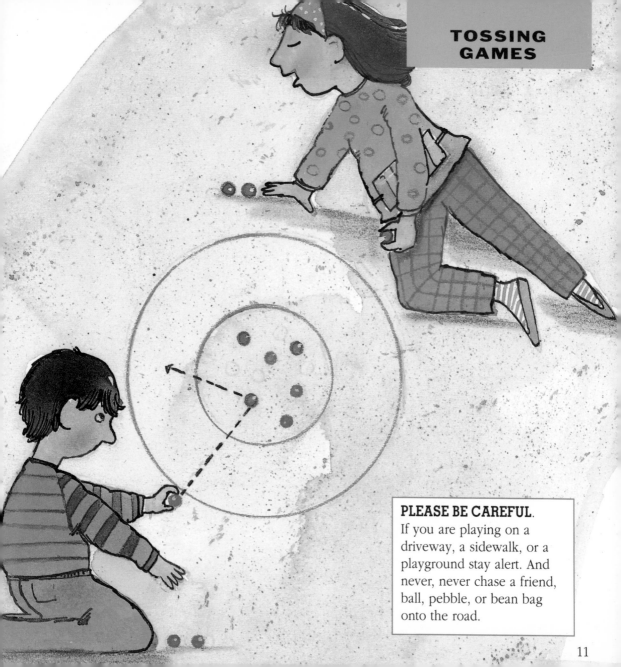

PLEASE BE CAREFUL. If you are playing on a driveway, a sidewalk, or a playground stay alert. And never, never chase a friend, ball, pebble, or bean bag onto the road.

CHALK ART

FLOOR PAINTING

Gather together: Colored chalk, dark colored construction paper, 1 cup (250 mL) water.

Dip the chalk into the water and draw on the pavement, playground, or even paper. The chalk will look waxy like pastels or sticky crayons. Once it dries it will not brush away easily.

KEEPSIES DRAWING

Gather together: Colored construction paper, an individual serving of plain yogurt, colored chalk.

With your fingers, smear dark colored construction paper with yogurt. Draw through the yogurt onto the paper with chalk. Let it dry. The yogurt fixes the chalk to the paper and the chalk will not rub off.

WINDOW CHALK

Add 2 teaspoons (10 mL) dish washing liquid to 1/4 cup (60 mL) liquid tempera paint in a bowl.

Decorate windows with hearts on Valentine's day, flowers in the spring, and Santa during the winter holidays. Once the holiday is over, the window is easy to clean.

CHALK TIP

After you have made your works of art, hang them up on a clothes line and invite your friends to your art show. You may even want to have some extra chalk on hand and have a chalk drawing party.

SPOT THE ROCK

Imagine decorating your neighborhood with art. Creating street art is simple but you'll need supplies. First, find one adult willing to help. Second, you may need a wagon. Third, you'll want several colors of chalk.

Walk around and spot some not-too-heavy rocks. Make sure the rocks are not on private property. Load them onto your wagon and take them home to decorate with colored chalk. Remember, never draw any words or pictures on the rocks that would hurt people's feelings. Pictures work best.

Load them back onto your wagon and use them to decorate your neighborhood. You may need an adult to help you pick appropriate spots for your art-rocks. If the rocks are very big you may want to decorate the rocks on the spot.

COME TO OUR ROCK PARTY

BASIC HOPSCOTCH (POTSY)

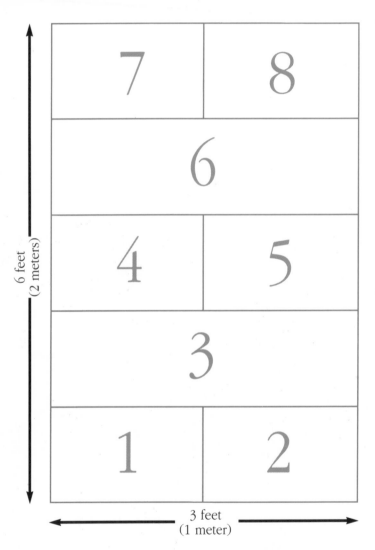

6 feet (2 meters)

3 feet (1 meter)

Age: 4 and up

Players: 2 or more

Materials: Chalk and a small pebble or token (called the "pot") for each child

• Draw your hopscotch board on a small or medium surface.

• To begin, player 1 tosses her pot onto 1. She then hops on her RIGHT foot into 2 and then into 3 (staying on her right foot). She then jumps so that her LEFT foot lands in 4 and her RIGHT foot lands in 5. Next she jumps so she lands with her RIGHT foot in 6 followed by another jump so that her LEFT foot lands on 7 and her RIGHT foot in 8.

• Now it's time to return.

• She must now jump and turn around so that she lands with her RIGHT foot in 7 and her LEFT foot in 8. She then hops so that her LEFT foot lands in 6 and then again so that she lands with her LEFT foot in 5 and her RIGHT foot in 4. She then jumps on her LEFT foot into 3 and then 2. When she has reached 2, she leans over and picks up the pot and hops out of the field.

• If she has been successful, she tosses her pot into 2 and repeats the steps. A player loses her turn if she steps on a line, trips, or tosses the pot onto the wrong square. When this happens it is the next player's turn.

• The game is over when one player has successfully gone through all the numbers on the board.

DID YOU KNOW that hopscotch is a very old game played by children of many different nations and cultures? The remains of hopscotch boards can still be seen today carved into the streets of ancient Rome.

HOPSCOTCH-IN-THE-ROUND

Age: 3 and up

Players: 2 or more

Materials Chalk and pebbles

• Draw your choice of hopscotch board on a small surface or sidewalk.

• Stand with both feet on the start line. Toss the pebble to the second circle and jump ON BOTH FEET onto circle 1.

• Now lean way over and pick up the pebble on circle 2. Toss the pebble to circle 3 and jump ON BOTH FEET to circle 2. Keep going. If your pebble bounces out of a circle, if you lose your balance, if you put a hand down on the ground then, whoops — it's back to the beginning.

COOPERATIVE VERSION:

Draw animals in each circle. When you land on the circle act and sound like the animal you are standing on.

DID YOU KNOW that during the Great Depression (1929 to 1939), hobos — men who traveled the country in search of work — carried bits of chalk in their pockets? They went door to door asking for food. If someone was kind and gave them food, the hobo would leave a small chalk mark near the door or on the curb near the house. If the people inside were unkind, the hobo would leave a different mark. Other hobos passing through would then know if this home was a place where they could receive comfort.

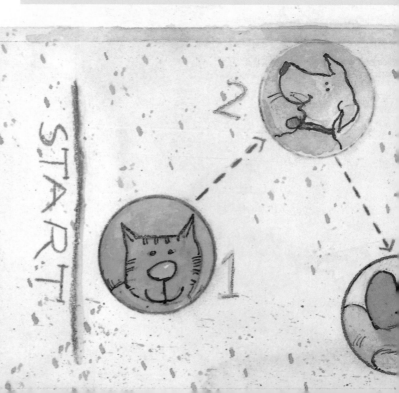

TWEET

COOPERATIVE HOPSCOTCH

Age: 4 and up

Players: 2 or more

Materials: Chalk

• Draw your hopscotch board on a small surface.

• Pick one person who will toss and pick up the pot. Toss the pot onto 1. Stand beside each other with your arms around each other's waists.

• Together, hop on one foot to the second square. Then to the next.

• Hop all the way to the rest square. Put both feet down and turn around. Put your arms around each other's waists again. Now hop back to the second space, pick up the pot, and hop off the board. Toss the pot to the second square and start again.

• If one of the players steps on a line or puts two feet down, then everyone must go back to the beginning.

REST SPACE

CHINESE HOPSCOTCH

Age: 5 and up
Players: 2 or more
Materials: Chalk and pebbles

• Draw your board on a small surface.

8
7
6
5
4
3
2
1

• Stand on one foot at the start line and kick the pebble to 1 with the other foot.

• If the pebble lands and stays in 1, then hop onto 1. Stand on one foot and kick the pebble to 2.

• Remember, stand on one foot at all times. If both feet touch the ground then go back to the end of the line and let another player try.

DID YOU KNOW that in China today entire schools have great competitions using this game?

20

WALK IN THE WOODS

Pack enough chalk for everyone to use when you go on your next trip into the woods. Mark the trees as you go along. On your way back the smallest member of your trekking group can lead the way home. No matter what, don't ever go into the woods without an adult.

TAKARATORI

Age: 7 and up

Players: 6 or more

Materials: Chalk and 2 twigs or sticks

• This game is from Japan. "Takara" means treasure and "tori" means get or catch.

• Draw a 25-foot (8-meter) long "S" with chalk on a large surface. Place a stick on home base at either end of the "S." The stick is the takara. Draw several circles or "islands" around the S. Draw a straight line through the middle of the S to divide the two teams.

• The object is to capture the other team's treasure. After dividing into two teams, one at each end of the "S," the players stand on one foot and hop over the field toward the opposite end to capture the takara. While hopping, players try to tag members of the other team. Players may put both feet down to rest only on an island. When another player from either team arrives at the island, the player there must hop off.

• If one player tags another, they play Jankenpon (see next page) while the other players keep hopping. The winner of Jankenpon keeps playing and the loser steps to the side and cheers everyone else. The game is over when one team captures the other team's treasure.

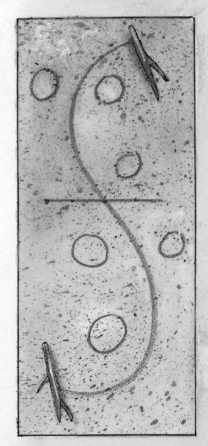

JANKENPON

• Two players face each other. They each have one hand behind their back. Then, together, they call out "Jankenpon." On "pon," they bring their hands from behind their backs and display one of the following:

• A clenched fist – the "rock."

• An open hand with flat palm – the "paper."

• Two fingers (index and middle fingers) pointing out – the "scissors."

Paper beats rock because paper can wrap around a rock.

Scissors beats paper because scissors can cut paper.

Rock beats scissors because a rock can smash a pair of scissors.

FOUR CORNER UPSET

Age: 5 and up
Players: 5
Materials: Chalk

• The game is played on a large playing area or closed-off intersection.

• One player who is "IT" stands in the middle. The other players stand on the corners.

IT calls out, "I want a corner. Give me yours," while pointing to one corner.

• Chances are no one will give up a corner, so IT yells out, "I'm upset." All the corners run to the right.

IT tries to get to a corner before one of the other players. If IT gets there first, the player without a corner becomes IT. Careful, IT may try to fool the other players by yelling out, "I'm UPSIDE-DOWN" instead of "I'm UPSET." A runner might move off a corner with nowhere to go and IT may claim her spot.

25 feet
(approx. 8 meters)

ALTERNATIVE: If you only have four players, draw a triangle instead of a square. IT stands in the middle of the triangle and the other three children stand on the points of the triangle.

FOX AND GEESE

Age: 5 and up
Players: 5 or more
Materials: Chalk

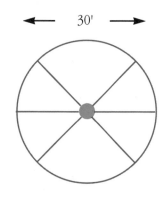

← 30' →

• Draw a circle about 30 feet (10 meters) across on a large surface. Divide it into pie-shaped sections as illustrated. Mark home base.

• One player is the Fox. The rest of the players are Geese. The Fox has to catch all the Geese by tagging them. The Geese and the Fox may run in any direction but must stay on the chalk lines.

• The Geese can rest at home base and can not be tagged there. But only one Goose can be on home base at a time. When a new Goose arrives, any Goose already on home base must leave.

• Any Goose tagged by the Fox is out of the game and must leave the circle. The game is over when the Fox has captured all the Geese. Then, choose a new Fox and play the game again.

DOLLHOUSE

Imagine that your home is cut in half from top to bottom. On a small surface or chalkboard, draw all the rooms in your home and make your own dollhouse. Decorate your dollhouse with miniature furniture or tables and beds made out of little sticks and stones. Add a doll or two and an instant dollhouse is created for the day. You may even wish to add a few rooms — how about a sunroom or playroom?

Make your own
CHALKBOARD

Chalkboard paint can be found at most hardware stores in two colors — green or black. Buy a small sheet of Masonite (plywood or pressboard will also do) and give the smooth surface two or three coats of paint. Make a chalk trough by nailing or gluing a strip of molding to the bottom of the board.

DOTS AND LINES

Age: 6 and up

Players: 2

Materials: Chalk

• On a small chalkboard or small hard surface draw rows of dots. There should be the same number of dots on each side of the square. Decide who goes first.

• Player 1 joins two dots with a line. Player 2 then joins two dots with a line. Dots can only be joined up and down or sideways, not diagonally.

• Take turns drawing lines until one player completes a square. That player prints an initial or a mark inside the square. The player who completes a square goes again.

• The game is over when all the dots have been joined and all the squares have been claimed. The player with the most squares wins.

• If you want to make this game last longer, make the square bigger by adding more dots. Try a game with a 100 dots, 10 dots long and 10 dots wide.

TIC-TAC-TOE

Age: 5 and up
Players: 2
Materials: Chalk

• Draw the playing board on a chalkboard or small surface.

• Decide who will go first. Player 1 places an X in one of the nine spaces on the board.

• Player 2 places an O in one of the eight remaining spaces.

• The player who first gets 3 marks in a row, wins.

• The marks can go sideways, up and down, or on the diagonal. If no one wins, the players start over.

JARABADACH

This African game is like tic-tac-toe.

Age: 6 and up

Players: 2

Materials: Chalk and 6 tokens (3 each of a different color or shape)

• Draw your game board on a small surface.

• The nine numbered corners are the points of the square. Player 1 places a token on any of the nine points.

• Player 2 then places a token on one of the remaining points.

• Take turns until one player gets three tokens in a row and wins or all the tokens have been played.

• The three tokens can be sideways, up and down, or on the diagonal.

• If the six tokens have been played and no one has won, take turns moving the tokens along the lines, one space at a time, until one player wins.

NINE MEN'S MORRIS

Age: 9 and up

Players: 2

Materials: Chalk and 18 tokens (9 each of a different color or shape)

• Draw a square about 1 foot (30 cm) on each side on a small surface. Inside the big square draw a smaller square. Inside the smaller square draw an even smaller square.

• Next, draw four lines that join the corners of the three squares. Then draw four lines to join the middle of each side of the three squares, as in the illustration.

• Players begin the game by taking turns putting their tokens on one of the 24 points on the board where lines meet.

• Each player tries to get three tokens on the board in a row along a line. When all of the tokens have been placed on the board, the players take turns moving one token at a time directly from one point to another open point to make three in a row.

• The object of the game is to remove as many of the other player's tokens as possible. At any time in the game, when a player has made three in a row, that player may remove one of the other player's tokens from the board.

• The game is over when one player has only two tokens left on the board or cannot make any more moves. When this happens, the other player wins.

> **DID YOU KNOW** this is a very old game from England? It was even played by William Shakespeare. He mentions it in his play, *A Midsummer Night's Dream* (Act II, Scene I). See if you can find the passage.

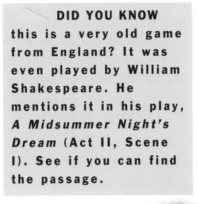

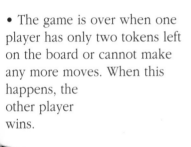

FIGHTING SERPENTS

Age: 9 and up

Players: 2

Materials: Chalk, ruler, and 44 tokens (22 tokens per player). Each player uses a different color or shape. The Aztecs used painted plum pits.

• Draw three lines, one above the other, about 30 inches (75 cm) long and 4 inches (10 cm) apart on a small surface.

• Take the ruler and mark a dot every 2 inches (5 cm) along the top and bottom line. (Try to mark the first dots on each line so that they are directly above and below each other.)

• Draw a line joining the first dot on the top line to the second dot on the bottom line.

• Draw another line from the second dot on the top line to the third dot on the bottom line. Continue this for all the dots along the top line.

• Do the same for the bottom line. Join the first dot on the bottom line to the second dot on the top line. Do this for all the dots along the bottom line.

• Each player places all of her tokens on her side of the board and randomly in the middle so that all of the dots are covered on all three lines except three. The only dots that are not covered are the two outside dots on the middle line and the central dot on the middle line.

• Play begins with player 1 moving one token along a line to any of the three open spaces.

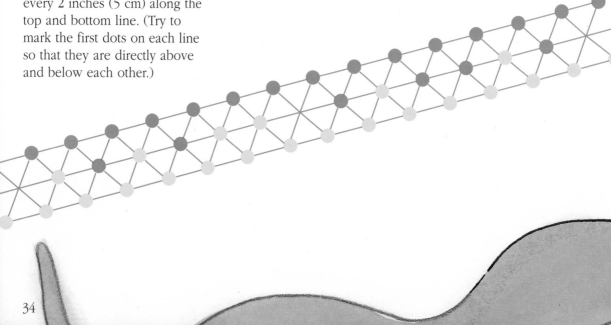

34

• Then player 2 moves. A player captures a token by jumping over it to an empty dot beyond it in the same direction.

• When a token is captured it is removed from the board.

• A player must capture a token when possible, even if other moves are open. If a player is unable to capture one of the other player's tokens, she may move one of her own tokens one space to an open dot.

• The player who captures all of the opponent's tokens first wins.

WORD STREAM

Age: 8 and up
Players: 2 and up
Materials: Chalk

• In this game, the players create a "stream" of words on the chalkboard. Each word added to the stream is related to the word before it, based on a rule that the players have chosen.

• For example, the players might decide that each word must be four letters long and that each new word has to use three letters from the word before it. This means the player making the word can change only one letter in the previous word, but can scramble the letters.

• Here's an example.
tall – change the *t* to *b*
      to make:
ball – now change the *l* to *e*
      and scramble to get:
able – change the *b* to *d*
      and scramble to make:
lead – change the *e* to *i*
      and make *dial.*

• When players are unable to make a word, they are out. The last player to make a word wins. Players might help each other to make the longest stream possible.

• Here's another idea. Choose a subject. Use the last letter of each word to make a new word.

• For example if the subject is animals, the word stream might look like this:
    cat
    tiger
    rabbit
    tarantula
    antelope
    elephant

• Other subjects might be first names, fruits, countries, and so on.

CAR RALLY

Would you make a good racing car driver? Car Rally is a test of driving skill and car performance.

Age: 6 and up

Players: 2 to 6

Materials: Chalk and one toy car for each player

• Rally your cars on a fairly smooth, small surface.

RALLY 1 — Car Curling

• The players stand behind the start line and take turns rolling the cars from behind the start line toward the center of the bull's-eye.

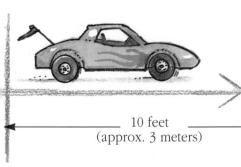

• The car scores the number of points in the circle where it stops. If a car stops on a line with part of the car in one space and part of the car in another space, the space with the higher score counts. If a car stops outside all of the circles, no points are scored. If any part of the car touches the small center dot, score ten points.

• Each player gets a warm-up turn and four counting turns. The highest score after four rolls wins Rally 1.

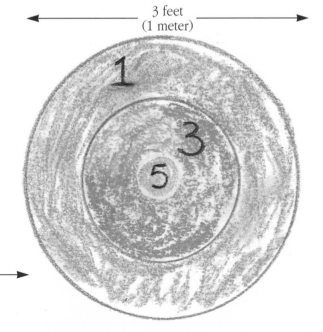

10 feet
(approx. 3 meters)

3 feet
(1 meter)

37

CAR RALLY

RALLY 2 — Two Hands on the Wheel

• Each driver rolls a car from behind the start line into the middle lane as straight as possible.

• Cars that curve away into the other lanes score the points for the lane where they stop. Cars that stop on a line get the score of the lane with higher points.

• If the car misses any of the lanes or goes beyond the end of the board, no points are scored.

• Each driver gets one warm-up turn and four counting turns. The highest score after four rolls wins Rally 2.

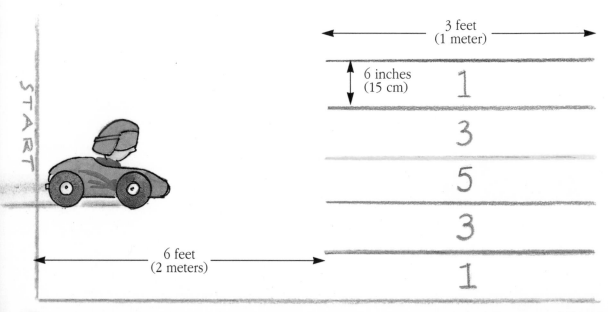

START

3 feet
(1 meter)

6 inches
(15 cm)

1

3

5

3

1

6 feet
(2 meters)

RALLY 3 — Slam on the Brakes

• Each driver rolls a car from behind the start line. The driver scores the number of points awarded to the space where the car stops.

• If the car stops on a line, the score of the higher space counts. If a car does not cross the first line or if it goes beyond the end line, no points are scored.

• If a car does not stop on the board, no points score.

• Each driver gets one warm-up turn and four counting turns. The highest score after four rolls wins Rally 3.

RALLY GRAND CHAMPION

After all three rallies have been run, each driver adds up the total score for all three events. The driver with the highest score becomes the Grand Champion Rally Driver.

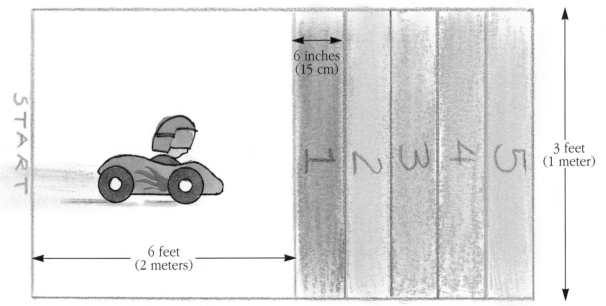

6 inches (15 cm)

3 feet (1 meter)

6 feet (2 meters)

TWISTIE

Age: 5 and up

Players: 3 or 4

Materials: Chalk and a pair of dice

• Draw this game on a small surface.

• For a three-player game draw 12 small circles in a six-foot (two meter) space. (For a four-player game use 18 circles.)

• Number each circle from 1 to 6. Each number will be used in at least two circles.

• Player 1 rolls the dice. If, for example, one die says "6," put one foot on a circle 6. If the second die says "3," put the other foot on a circle 3. Player 2 takes a turn. If a circle is already taken, roll the die until an open space is found.

• Continue until everyone has both their feet on the board.

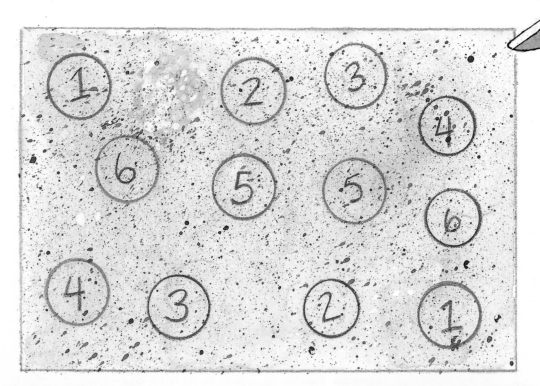

- Player 1 then rolls again. This time the dice tell where to place the hands.

- Players are eliminated when they lose their balance and fall over.

- If everyone has been able to place both hands and feet on the circles without falling, everyone raises one foot. Whoever falls is out.

- Anyone left lifts a hand. This continues until one player is left – the winner.

VARIATION: If there are no dice handy, write the numbers one to six on pieces of paper and designate a player as the "Number Picker" to draw the number from a hat.

ALTERNATIVE: Odd roll = feet, even roll = hands.

MINI-MINI PUTT

Age: 7 and up

Players: 2 to 4

Materials: Chalk, a large marble, one Popsicle stick, and one small marble for each player

• Play golf on a fairly smooth surface.

• Player 1 places a ball (small marble) on the "tee," which is the starting point for the golf ball. He hits the ball with his Popsicle "club."

• Then it's player 2's turn. When all of the players have had their first shot, player 1 takes his second.

• Players take turns until everyone has finished the hole.

• The object is to hit the ball from the tee and strike the hole ball (large marble) using as few strokes as possible. The player who uses the fewest strokes wins.

• There is one other rule to remember. If a ball goes outside the oval chalk line, it is out of bounds and costs an extra stroke. When this happens the ball is placed on the chalk line where it went out and the next shot is taken from there.

6 feet
(2 meters)

6 inches
(15 cm)

3 feet
(1 meter)

TEE **X**

VARIATIONS ON MINI-MINI PUTT

Design some really wacky golf holes like these.

Place obstacles like running shoes or toy cars in the middle of the course. The ball now has to be hit around them in order to get a clear shot at the hole ball. Penalties can be added for hitting some obstacles and perhaps points can be awarded for hitting others. The possibilities are endless.

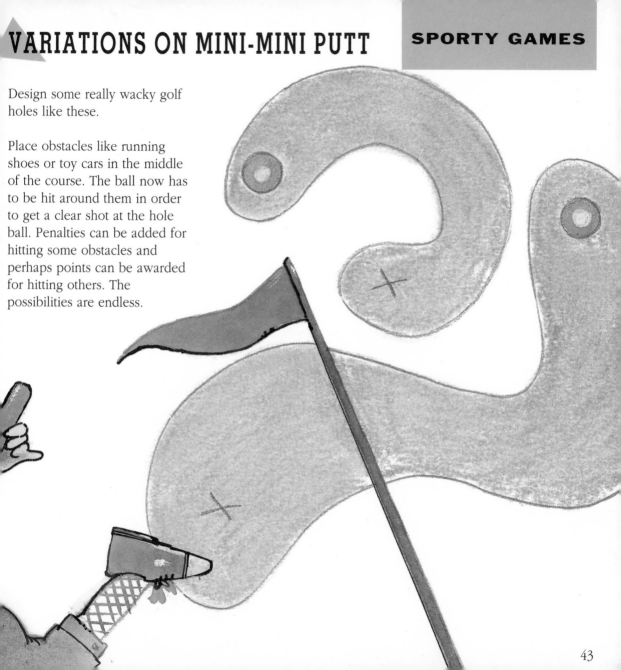

43

CHALK CITY

With your teacher's help, and your principal's permission, throw a Chalk-Around-The-Block party on the playground at your school.

Imagine what your town would look like from the air. Draw in the streets. Each child in your class, or school, may draw in their homes or apartment buildings. Where is the fire hall? Police station? Shops? You might even take your red chalk and mark off "no-go" areas such as parking lots, building sites, or heavily wooded areas.

HUMAN SUNDIAL

On a sunny day, early in the morning, stand in the middle of a playground or driveway. Ask a friend to draw an outline of your shadow with chalk. Draw an outline of your feet, too. Print the time beside the shadow drawing.

Wait a few hours and do a second shadow drawing. Remember to stand in exactly the same place. Print the time of day beside the shadow.

At noon do a third shadow drawing. Where does your shadow fall?

Do as many shadow drawings as you wish throughout the day. See how the sun moves? Now you will be able to tell the approximate time by your shadow.

MINI QUIZ

Each of these people or activities uses chalk.
Can you tell how and why they use chalk?
(The answers are on the next page.)

1.

2.

3.

4.

5.

6.

7.

8.

9.

ANSWERS:

1) Teachers use chalkboards and chalk to teach their students. Many years ago students used chalk and small chalkboards instead of pencils and paper. The small chalkboards were made from a type of rock called slate. Paper was very expensive and hard to come by.

2) Darts players record their scores with chalk on small chalkboards. If you go into a pub in England, Ireland, or Scotland you would see the dart board and the chalkboard.

3) Police officers mark the tires of parked cars with chalk. If the car is still there when the officers next pass, they recognize it and know approximately how long the car has been parked.

4) Rock climbers rub their hands with powdered chalk to give them extra grip while climbing a rock face or mountain.

5) Actors have to move to certain areas on the stage at specific times during performances. During rehearsals the director marks the stage with chalk to show the actor where to go.

6) Gymnasts often rub powdered chalk on their hands before mounting the parallel bars or the vault. Many floor gymnasts use chalk on their feet for extra grip.

7) Tailors and dressmakers use chalk to mark parts of the cloth that must be taken in or hemmed.

8) Pool players take a small square of chalk and "chalk-up" their pool cue before and during a game. This gives the player more control over his shots.

9) Dancers in the ballet often dip their toe shoes in powdered chalk to give them extra grip and help prevent them from slipping.